Animal Survival

ANIMAL SENSES

Michel Barré

Gareth Stevens Publishing
MILWAUKEE

— The author wishes to thank Jack Guichard and Maurice Berteloot for their encouragement, critiques, and advice during the writing of this book.

The U.S. editor would like to extend special thanks to Jan W. Rafert, Curator of Primates and Small Mammals, Milwaukee County Zoo, Milwaukee, Wisconsin, for his kind and professional help with the information in this book.

For a free color catalog describing Gareth Stevens' list of high-quality books and multimedia programs, call 1-800-542-2595 (USA) or 1-800-461-9120 (Canada). Gareth Stevens Publishing's Fax: (414) 225-0377.
See our catalog, too, on the World Wide Web: http://gsinc.com

Library of Congress Cataloging-in-Publication Data

Barré, Michel, 1928-
  [Sens chez les animaux. English]
  Animal senses / by Michel Barré.
    p. cm. — (Animal survival)
  Includes bibliographical references (p. 47) and index.
  Summary: Discusses how different animals use their senses to find
food, attract a mate, detect danger, bond with their young, and more.
  ISBN 0-8368-2078-9 (lib. bdg.)
  1. Senses and sensation—Juvenile literature. 2. Animal behavior—
Juvenile literature. [1. Senses and sensation. 2. Animals—Physiology.]
  I. Title. II. Series: Barré, Michel, 1928- Animal survival.
  QP434.B37 1998
  573.8'7—dc21   97-40158

This North American edition first published in 1998 by
Gareth Stevens Publishing
1555 North RiverCenter Drive, Suite 201
Milwaukee, Wisconsin 53212 USA

This U.S. edition © 1998 by Gareth Stevens, Inc. Original © 1995 by Éditions MANGO-Éditions PEMF, under the French title *Les sens chez les animaux.* Additional end matter © 1998 by Gareth Stevens, Inc.

Translated from the French by Janet Neis.
U.S. editor: Rita Reitci
Editorial assistant: Diane Laska

Series consultant: Michel Tranier, zoologist at the French National Museum of Natural History.

The editors wish to thank the Jacana Agency, and the artists who kindly granted permission to use the photographs displayed in the following pages:

Cover, Varin-Visage, C. K. Lorenz, A. Larivière; 4, F. Pölking; 5, A. Shah; 6, W. Wisniewski; 7, A. Shah; 8, Cosmos/E. Ferorelli; 9, J. Lepore; 10, Varin-Visage; 11, J.-P. Ferrero; 12, J.-P. Varin; 13, F. Gohier; 14, N. Wu; 15, H. Chaumeton, J.-P. Thomas; 16, H. Chaumeton; 17, F. Winner, J.-P. Heruy; 18, J.-F. Hellio-N. Van Ingen; 19, Rouxaine, J.-P. Varin; 20, A. Bougrain-Dubourg; 21, Frédéric; 22, Y. Arthus-Bertrand; 23, J. Robert; 24, S. De Wilde; 25, Y. Lanceau, Ferrero-Labat; 26, M. Danegger; 28, J.-M. Labat; 29, A. Brosset; 30, H. Chaumeton, C. Morel; 31, M. Danegger, C. and M. Moiton; 32, Varin-Visage; 33, 34, J.-P. Varin; 35, M. Tuttle-PHR; 36, H. Chaumeton; 37, R. König, C. and M. Moiton; 38, J.-M. Labat; 39, A. Kerneis-Dragesco; 40, J.-F. Hellio-N. Van Ingen; 41, P. Pickford; 42, Bramaz-Jerrican; 43, P. Pilloud, W. Geiersperger; 44, Ferrero-Labat; 45, A. Ducrot, Y. Gillon

Printed in the United States of America

1 2 3 4 5 6 7 8 9 02 01 00 99 98

CONTENTS

KNOWING THE SURROUNDINGS   4

FINDING OR AVOIDING THE SAME SPECIES   6

HOW WE EXPLORE ANIMAL SENSES   8

THE WORLD OF SCENTS AND TASTES   10

DETECTING SCENTS IN WATER   12

SMELLING WITH TENTACLES   14

USING ANTENNAE TO SMELL   16

SEVERAL WAYS TO SMELL   18

MAMMALIAN SENSITIVITY TO SCENTS   20

SCENTS FOR REPRODUCTION IN MAMMALS   22

SMELLING CLOSE-UP BY TOUCHING   24

SENSING VIBRATIONS AND SOUNDS   26

HEARING WITH THE BODY   28

INVERTEBRATE HEARING   30

UNNOTICEABLE EARS   32

MAMMAL EARS WITH AURICLES   34

DIFFERENT WAYS OF SEEING   36

THE EYES OF VERTEBRATES   38

PROBLEMS WITH VISION   40

SEEING COLORS   42

SEEING WITH DIFFERENT EYES   44

GLOSSARY   46

BOOKS, VIDEOS, AND WEB SITES   47

INDEX   48

KNOWING THE SURROUNDINGS

Above: **An osprey catches a fish for its meal.**

Locating food

Before an animal that lives in the wild can eat, it must find food. A plant-eater often will recognize food by its appearance or smell. An animal that eats other animals must locate prey, too, before it can catch and kill it.

When searching for food, each species uses its senses of smell, sight, hearing, touch, and taste in different ways.

Avoiding capture

It's essential to find food, but all animals also need to avoid becoming the prey of predators that want to eat them.

In order to protect themselves, animals must be alert to approaching enemies. Usually, they can smell, hear, or see them coming.

Finding the way

It's not enough for an animal to be able to move around freely in the wild. It also must be able to find its way back to its home, its family, and the places where it is most likely to find a sufficient food supply.

Different species of animals usually find their way around in different ways — by smell, sight, or sound.

Migrating animals often have special senses that direct them along the correct path.

Below: **Zebras and antelopes fleeing a hunting lion.**

Finding or Avoiding the Same Species

Above: **A buck calls to gather the does of its herd and to warn off other bucks.**

Searching for a mate

Very few animals can produce young without the males and females of the species mating.

In order to attract male partners, some females send out a scent or, more rarely, a light signal. Some males attract their female partners by calling or singing, by displaying certain postures, by wearing certain colors, or by doing a "dance" to prepare for mating.

Both males and females of the same species must sense these signals in order to reproduce.

Rivals and relatives

Some animals do not share their space with others of the same species that may later become rivals. The animals mark their territories by sending out cries or songs and by chasing away intruders that enter their space. Animals living in groups recognize and drive away others that do not belong to their communities.

Animal parents in some species develop special relationships with their young during the time they feed them and teach them survival skills.

Scents, sounds, and even colors can play an important part in the relationships between animals that are of the same species. The ability to receive and understand these messages is critical for the survival of animal species. Without this communication, many animals would die out.

Below: **Family ties develop as a lioness licks her cubs.**

HOW WE EXPLORE
ANIMAL SENSES

Above: **Observing animals helps us understand them.**

Observing animals over the last several hundred years has taught humans many details of the ways in which animals live.

For example, for a long time, no one really knew whether or not animals could recognize colors or receive sounds the way humans do.

Finding out

In the last hundred years or so, close studies of animals have provided new and better information than ever before, so researchers now have some exact answers.

For instance, an animal is provided with good-tasting food on a red table, and bad-tasting food on a blue table. If the animal has trouble finding the good food after many repetitions, it probably means that the

animal either cannot tell the colors apart or keeps mixing them up.

If an animal reacts to a shape similar to something it recognizes, such as its mother or a predator, researchers can give the animal a decoy, and, by varying the details of the decoy, they can tell which features the animal can distinguish well and which ones it cannot.

This is how scientists discovered that baby gulls open their beaks when they see shapes that have a red spot but do not otherwise resemble the shape of the mother gull's beak.

When the same scientists covered the red spot on the mother's beak, the baby gulls did not react when their mother came near because they could no longer recognize her.

Sometimes, researchers create unusual conditions for the animals — such as changing their familiar environment or social activities — to see if and how the animals will react to these changes.

Scientific tools

Some machines allow humans to amplify and record animal messages that our eyes, ears, and noses cannot pick up.

Electronic equipment can produce sounds of different frequencies, including those that the human ear cannot detect.

Scientists studying the animals' reactions to the different sounds have been able to learn that some animals hear much better than humans. They also have found other animals that do not hear as well as we do.

The information in this book is the result of the patient work done by many dedicated, humane research teams.

A great deal of close study has been done. But we still have a lot to learn about the sensory world in which animals carry out their lives.

Above: **A wolf howls to communicate to distant wolves.**

Below: **Sound waves made visible by an oscilloscope.**

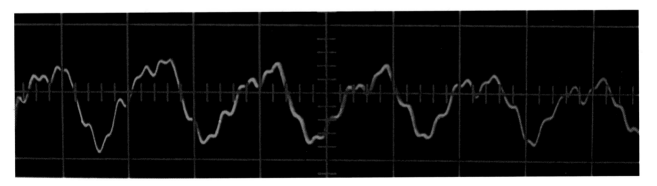

THE WORLD OF SCENTS AND TASTES

Above: **The kiwi is one of the few birds with a good sense of smell. It can sniff out earthworms.**

stuffs up a person's nose, food often seems to lose most of its flavor.

Humans are able to tell the difference between flavors, which need direct contact to detect, and scents, which can be detected from a distance. Many animals, however, are not able to tell the difference between them.

Using scents

The kiwi, a wingless bird from New Zealand, can detect the scent of an earthworm that is under the ground.

The blackbird, which also eats earthworms, guesses where they are by listening for the faint sounds they make as they dig through the earth.

American vultures have a good sense of smell, but the vultures in Asia and Africa do not. All vultures feed on dead carcasses. The smell of these decaying carcasses

For humans, the scents we smell with our noses differ from the flavors we taste with our tongues. Sense differences like these do not exist for many animals. Humans sometimes have trouble separating these senses. For example, when a cold

carries through the air. If a carcass is hidden in foliage, its scent can be tracked down easily by American vulture species, but the vultures in Asia and Africa, without the sense of smell, will fly right over it. If, however, the vultures see hyenas or jackals gathering around something, they know there is a carcass to eat and will fly down to claim their share of the food.

DETECTING SCENTS
IN WATER

Above: **This young pike smelled the smaller fish from a distance.**

Underwater scents

Research has shown that animals can detect scents under the water.

When scientists place a bitter substance onto the body of a small fish, a larger fish will be able to smell the smaller fish before it can actually see it. When the larger fish grabs its prey, however, it spits it out because of the bitter taste.

Smelling well

Fish are able to detect tiny differences in their home waters. These include the amounts of salt and other substances that may be present in the water, even when they exist in very small quantities. Fish usually use their sense of smell to find food and detect unwelcome predators.

After living in the sea for years, salmon return to mate in the rivers where their lives began. Guided by scent on their journey, they can recognize their home waters as long as pollution has not changed the river.

Below: **These salmon use their sense of smell to guide them to the Alaskan river of their birth.**

SMELLING WITH TENTACLES

Above: **Clown fish swim safely among the tentacles of a sea anemone.**

Simple animals use the same organs for touching and for detecting scents.

The sea anemone uses its tentacles to recognize the small crustaceans and fish it finds good to eat. It will eat most fish, but not the clown fish, which carries the same scent as the sea anemone.

Other fish, which do not carry the anemone's scent, are not protected. If they get too close, the anemone can paralyze and eat them.

Bivalve mollusks, such as the mussel and the oyster, open their shells to let in water. The water flow brings them oxygen

and the tiny algae and other microscopic organisms they eat.

Sometimes the bivalve mollusks close their shells quickly when they smell an approaching predator. When it claps together the two halves of its shell, a scallop can even move itself around.

The snail smells with the tiny tentacles on its head. From a distance, it can sense the moisture it needs. It can see with the eyes at the end of its large tentacles. Its foot can taste particles of food, which it then eats.

Below: **The snail smells with the two small tentacles at the front. The large tentacles have eyes on the ends.**

USING ANTENNAE TO SMELL

Above: **The spiny lobster uses its long antennae to smell.**

Crustaceans

Some crustaceans have antennae that allow them to smell. The antennae of shrimp and lobsters are very long. Crabs have much shorter antennae.

Insects

Insect antennae can be long or short, depending on the species. They can be shaped like threads, clubs, combs, or fans. Using their antennae, these animals recognize the plants they like from far away. This helps them lay their eggs on the plants that will be food for their young larvae.

The best insect smellers are moths, which have large, feathery antennae. When ready to mate, the female moths secrete a special scent from a gland in the abdomen. This scent attracts males from a distance of several miles (kilometers).

Jean-Henri Fabre, the famous insect researcher, captured a female moth and placed her in a black screen bell. In spite of the screen, the males gathered to try to reach the female. After taking the males away, Fabre put the female in a glass bell. Now the males could see her clearly, but they did not react this time because they couldn't smell her.

The female mosquito detects the heat that warm-blooded animals give off. She bites these animals and drinks their blood, which is needed to make her eggs hatch.

Above: **Like most insects, the grasshopper smells with its antennae.**

Below: **With its highly-developed antennae, this male moth can smell a female from far away.**

Several Ways to Smell

Above: **This viper's flicking tongue carries odors to its sense organs.**

Reptile sensors

Reptiles smell most scents the same way we do, by breathing through their nostrils.

Snakes and most lizards rapidly flick their tongues in and out, to pick up surrounding odors. The tongue transfers these odors to the roof of the mouth, which contains Jacobsen's organ. This extra organ is highly developed for detecting odors. It permits snakes to sense even the tiniest changes in odors; for example, prey moving into their neighborhood.

Some snakes possess special organs that, at a distance, can sense the body heat of prey, such as a mouse. These heat-sensing organs lie along the lips of some boas and pythons. In rattlesnakes and other pit vipers, these heat sensors lie in pits under their eyes.

Insects sensing

A quick touch tells a butterfly which flowers have nectar it can drink. If you drop a little sugar water on a butterfly's foot, its coiled proboscis will quickly unroll to drink it.

Bees and wasps, like many other insects, can taste with their feet and can smell with the hairs on their bodies.

In communal insects, such as bees and ants, each insect carries the scent of the hive or the anthill. The insects may not enter until guards at the entrance smell them with their antennae.

If something happens that alters an insect's scent, the guards would send the insect away.

Ant trails are marked with a scent produced by glands in the ants that passed on the trail earlier. Marking the trails this way keeps the other ants from getting lost. If one of the ants is attacked, it secretes a scent of alarm that keeps the others safely away.

Right: **If the butterfly unrolls its proboscis, that means it has smelled nectar with its feet.**

Below: **These South American ants carry leaves they have cut. If one of them is attacked, it will send out an odor to warn its companions on the same path.**

MAMMALIAN
SENSITIVITY TO SCENTS

Above: **Some dogs are trained to find the scent of people trapped in an avalanche.**

People who work in perfume manufacturing have a very good sense of smell and can distinguish the ingredients that make up perfume.

Dogs are forty times more sensitive to scents than humans are. This allows them to recognize and follow a person's path after smelling a piece of that person's clothing. This is how they can find people lost in a forest, in the mountains, or in an avalanche.

Dogs also can be trained to find hidden drugs and explosives. And hunting dogs know how to follow the trails of other animals.

Even without using such a strong sense of smell, mammals often are guided by scents.

We know that, in order to watch animals in the wild, we must approach them against the wind. If we don't, the wind will

carry our scent to them. Alarmed, the animals will run out of sight.

Scent glands

The peccary, a small mammal from South America that is related to pigs, has a scent gland on its back. By rubbing it against other peccaries from the time they are born, members of the peccary herd acquire a collective scent. Each animal can recognize the others in its group.

Deer, horses, and many other hoofed animals have similar glands near their eyes or on their cheeks. By nuzzling each other's head, they mark the other animal with their scent so they will recognize each other the next time they meet.

Most mammals have these scent glands, but they may be located in different places on their body. Dogs usually sniff each other to recognize the scent.

Above: **Horses rub muzzles to scent each other for future recognition.**

Scents for Reproduction in Mammals

Above: **A lion sniffs a lioness to find out if she is ready for mating.**

scent, nearby cats come to visit. The female cat also will react to an approaching male when she recognizes its scent.

For a long time, scientists could not determine exactly when female pigs, or sows, were ready to reproduce.

Then researchers discovered that by spraying a sow's muzzle with a scent similar to that of a male pig, or boar, the female would react in a way that signalled it was the right time to mate. If the time was not exactly right for mating, the sow would not react to the male scent.

Calling by scent

When female mammals are ready to mate, their glands secrete a certain scent. This scent attracts males of the same species.

For example, when a female cat is ready to mate and gives off the

Maternal ties

As soon as its young are born, the female mammal licks them all over for some time. She learns to recognize the scent of her young and gives them her scent. This is how, for example, a sheep can recognize its own young in a flock.

If something prevents a female mammal from licking her newborn right away, she no longer will recognize its scent and will refuse to nurse it.

For the same reason, a wild animal often will refuse to feed her baby if a human has found and handled it. She may not recognize its scent.

Below: **A ewe licks her lamb so that she will recognize it later.**

23

SMELLING CLOSE-UP BY TOUCHING

Above: **The octopus has tentacles that can touch and grab.**

Other organs are also sensitive to touch, such as the kind of tentacles that are used as arms. The octopus and the squid touch with their armlike tentacles and use them to explore the crevices in rocks to find crustaceans to eat.

Fish barbels

Some species of fish, such as the sturgeon, root around in the mud with their snout. The barbels, or feelers, on their jaws can sense tiny prey, such as worms or mollusks, which these sturgeon live on.

Mammal muzzles

Most mammals will touch one another with their projecting jaws and nose, or muzzle. The muzzle can both smell and touch. Monkeys and raccoons, however, touch with their sensitive hands and feet.

Humans have sensitive skin, especially on the hands. For us, touching is very different from the other senses.

Animals have different ways of touching. Many of them have tentacles and antennae, sense organs that can smell things at a distance and also touch objects nearby.

Cat whiskers

If someone gently places a hand near the head of a sleeping cat, without even touching it, the cat's whiskers will move to find out what is happening. Without whiskers, the cat would not be able to sense a mouse approaching in the dark.

Other members of the cat family, such as lions, tigers, and leopards, use their whiskers in the same way. They can detect the smallest vibrations with their whiskers.

Above: **The sturgeon uses its barbels to find mollusks and worms in the mud.**

Below: **The elephant's trunk is strong and very sensitive.**

Elephant trunk

The elephant's trunk is its lengthened nose and upper lip. The animal has an excellent sense of smell. The strong trunk can seize objects, and the sensitive lobes at the tip act like fingers.

When the elephant uses its trunk to eat, it grasps foliage with the trunk and brings it to its mouth. The elephant also uses its trunk to drink. It sucks up large amounts of water into the trunk and squirts it into its open mouth.

SENSING VIBRATIONS AND SOUNDS

Above: **The hare's ears catch the slightest warning sound.**

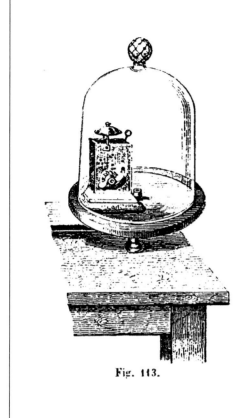

Fig. 113.

How a vacuum affects sounds

We can hear sounds only if they pass through a medium, or substance, that can vibrate in our bodies. The usual medium is air, but gas, vapors, liquids, and solids also can carry sound.

The following experiment shows that a medium needs to be present for sound to exist. Under a glass bell jar, a hammer powered by clockwork strikes a bell.

When the glass bell jar is full of air at ordinary pressure, you easily can hear the sound of the bell. If the air is pumped out so that a vacuum forms inside the bell jar, you no longer can hear the bell.

This experiment shows that sound does not travel in a vacuum.

Sounds of all types are actually vibrations that travel to our ears. These vibrations can start in many ways, such as by plucking a guitar string or striking a tuning fork. All other instruments and the voice make sound vibrations, too.

Vibrations cannot travel in a vacuum, but they can travel through water and even through solids. Early humans, when hunting, often located their prey by putting their ears to the ground and listening for the sound of running hooves.

Hearing sounds means sensing vibrations, but ears are not the only way that we sense vibrations.

We can experiment by plugging our ears when someone plays a bass drum or a tambourine nearby. Other parts of the body will detect the strong beats that come from these instruments.

Above: **An experiment with sound, taken from an old science text.**

HEARING WITH THE BODY

Above: **The lateral line is visible on the body of this freshwater fish.**

Fish can hear

Fish do not have any visible auditory canals through which sounds can enter. Because of this, scientists thought for a long time that fish just could not hear.

External sounds bounce off the surface of the water. Yet, if you tap your foot on the river bank, you will see the fish dart away. This shows that they heard the noise.

A fish has a lateral line along the length of its body. This line is very sensitive to the vibrations traveling through the water. A fish even can hear the movement of another fish.

A shark usually does not attack large prey. But when it picks up the vibrations of a frightened or injured animal, it knows it can attack without much risk. This is why human divers who stay calm when seeing a shark are less likely to be attacked than those who struggle or try to fight off the shark.

Reptiles feel sound

In India and Africa, some musicians charm snakes, making it look as if the animals are reacting to the music. Actually, snakes do not have any auditory canals, but they are not completely deaf.

They sense vibrations in the air and in the ground. These vibrations are then amplified in their bony skeletons, which connect to their internal ears at the jaw.

Below: **This cobra doesn't really hear the music, but its body feels the vibrations.**

29

INVERTEBRATE HEARING

Above: **Caterpillars feel sound vibrations with the tiny hairs on their bodies.**

Crustaceans don't have ears, but they can pick up sound vibrations through the sensitive hairs on their bodies. Caterpillars also use the hairs on their bodies for detecting sound vibrations.

Many insects, including grasshoppers and locusts, can sense sounds with their antennae or with sensitive hairs on their bodies. Cockroaches and crickets have filaments on their abdomens to detect any sound vibrations around them.

Male mosquitoes use their antennae to pick up the sounds made by female mosquitoes. Male antennae can receive only these particular sounds.

A spider's tiny feet can sense even the slightest vibrations of its web. When an insect that is trapped in the web tries to free itself, its struggles make vibrations that alert the spider.

Right: **The male mosquito uses its antennae to track down the sounds of a female.**

Left: The spider's sensitive feet tell it when something is happening anywhere in its web.

Left: This cricket senses sound using filaments on its abdomen.

31

UNNOTICEABLE EARS

Above: **A cricket makes its characteristic sound by rubbing its elytra together.**

The sensitivity of these organs varies, but they often let the insect hear ultrasounds — sounds at a higher pitch than humans can hear.

Double eardrums

Besides antennae and hairs, many insects have other auditory organs. Each organ contains a tiny eardrum with two membranes, or tympani. Between these tympani lie sensitive cells that pick up vibrations.

These organs can be found on the abdomens of cicadas and locusts, on the legs of grasshoppers and crickets, and on the thorax of some moths.

Without auricles

Amphibians, such as the frog and the toad, have a large eardrum behind each eye.

Birds have ears, but the auditory canal, the tube through which sounds enter, often is hidden by the bird's feathers.

Only nocturnal birds of prey, such as owls, have tufts of feathers that draw the slightest noises into the ear. Being able to hear their prey's smallest movements helps them hunt at night.

Birds are very sensitive to high-pitched sounds, but they are not as good at hearing low-pitched sounds and the ultrasounds that can be heard by an owl.

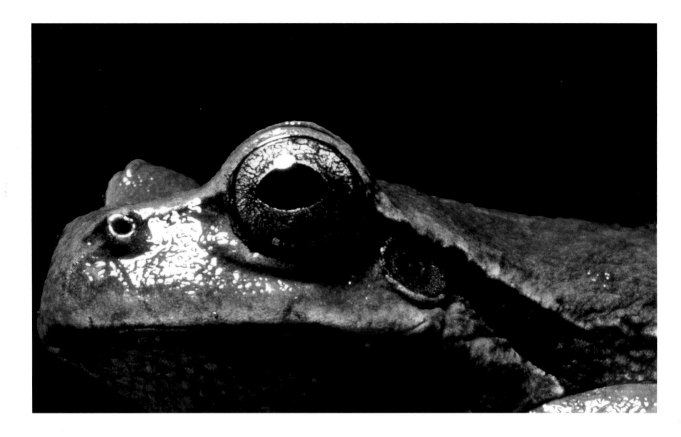

Above: The ear of the tree frog is the round membrane behind its eye.

Right: The horned owl's ears are on the side of its head. The tufts of feathers that form its "horns" amplify the sounds.

MAMMAL EARS WITH AURICLES

Above: **This African fennec fox uses its large ears to hear the slightest noise. It can find rodents quickly.**

Auricles can be very large and they are very important in the lives of fennecs, elephants, and several bat species. Most mammals can pivot their auricles, aiming them toward the sources of the sounds they detect so they can hear better.

A range of sounds

Dolphins and porpoises do not have auricles, but they are able to detect sounds well. They can even hear ultrasounds. Cats and dogs can also hear ultrasounds. Police dogs are specially trained to obey the sound of an ultrasound whistle.

Bats are able to hear the echoes of their own shrill cries, which bounce back from objects. This is called echolocation and explains how bats navigate so well at night, avoiding obstacles and finding prey.

Land mammals have auricles, structures that are outside the ear, which gather sounds and aim them into the auditory canal to the eardrum. Auricles help in hearing. If we increase the size of our auricles by cupping our hands behind our ears, we can hear better.

Above: **This bat pounces on an insect it has located in the darkness by using ultrasound echoes.**

DIFFERENT WAYS OF SEEING

Above: **Tiny, silvery "pearls" on the upper edge of this scallop are the sensitive cells used as eyes.**

Cells to see by

Bivalve mollusks can detect light with special cells on their bodies near the edges of their shells.

Snails have these special cells on the ends of their antennae. Earthworms have them along the length of their bodies.

The eel has them on the skin of its tail and can see even when its long body is completely hidden.

Primitive eyes

The ocellus is a fold of skin filled with a kind of gelatin that magnifies and sends images to the light-sensitive cells that are located at the back of the fold. This simple eye has blurred vision.

Caterpillars have ocelli, but when they become butterflies, they also will have compound eyes.

Many spiders have six or eight ocelli. They can see all around them, but not very clearly.

Poor vision

Although the mole is not completely blind, it can see very little.

Some insects, shrimp, salamanders, and fish that live in continual darkness, such as in underground caves or at the bottom of the sea, cannot see. By living without light for a long time, they have lost the organs for seeing.

Compound eyes

In addition to their small ocelli, most insects have compound eyes, which are large, round eyes with many facets. Crustaceans, such as the lobster and the crab, also can have them at the ends of their antennae.

A compound eye is made up of many tiny tubes, each sending its own tiny image. There are 5,000 facets in a bee's eye and up to 30,000 in the eye of a dragonfly.

Each tube has its own lens on top and a retinal cell at the bottom. The entire unit is surrounded by pigment cells to keep light in that unit. Each tube sees only that one visual spot.

The visual information received by all these tiny tubes is combined by the animal's brain into one image. Compound eyes are able to follow quick movements accurately.

Above: **The several simple eyes, or ocelli, on this spider's head do not see clearly. They mainly detect motion.**

Right: **This dragonfly has two large compound eyes, each made of thousands of tiny facets.**

THE EYES OF VERTEBRATES

Above: **The pupil in a cat's eye is narrow during the day but becomes round at night.**

brain, which interprets the image. It is actually the brain that "sees."

In bright light, the iris, a circular muscle around the pupil, can reduce this opening to let in less light. In dim light, the pupil gets larger to let in more light so the animal can see better.

Many animals have round pupils. Nocturnal hunters, such as the owl, have pupils that get very large in order to take in even the smallest amount of light. The cat's pupils form a narrow oval in the daytime. At night, they get larger and rounder.

In some snakes, the shark, and the octopus, the pupils can close into tiny slits.

The octopus and the squid, although they are both mollusks, have eyes much like vertebrate eyes. These two animals are the only invertebrates that can see actual shapes.

Every vertebrate eye contains a transparent crystalline lens. This lens focuses the image seen on the retina at the back of the eye, where many thousands of tiny cells transmit the sensations of light and color to the

Seeing far and near

In many animals, the lens bulges to varying degrees in order to focus sharply on objects near and far. This change is called accommodation.

Fish cannot change the shape of their spherical lens. Instead, the lens moves closer to or farther from the retina, similar to the way a camera focuses. Some fish that hunt near the surface, such as trout, use vision instead of smell to find insects that fly above the water.

Above: **The pupil of this tree viper can narrow down to a thin vertical line.**

Great vision

Birds' eyes are relatively large compared with other vertebrates. The ostrich eye is four times larger than the horse eye.

A larger eye means a larger number of sensitive cells in the retina. For example, there are eight times more cells in the retina of a sparrowhawk than in a human retina.

The part of the bird's brain devoted to vision is much larger than in other animals. Brain and eyes help explain why birds have such good vision.

Below: **The ostrich's large eyes give it excellent vision.**

PROBLEMS WITH VISION

Above: **The heron can catch its prey only when it aims next to where it sees the prey.**

The spherical lens of a fish eye sees correctly under water, but it would be nearsighted if used out of water.

The cormorant is a bird that hunts fish under water. When it dives into the water to look for a meal, the lenses of its eyes change shape and become spherical. The bird then can see in the water to hunt prey.

Frogs and some fish that climb on the roots of trees in the marsh have bulging eyes. This shape improves their vision out of water.

Seeing in water

Light rays do not travel in water the way they do in air. If part of a stick is put into water, it will appear broken when seen from outside the water. To see under the water the same as in the air, divers wear a face mask to trap some air in front of their eyes so light can go through.

Shifting aim

The heron keeps its head out of the water when it fishes. If it struck with its beak where it saw a fish, it would hit next to its prey. So the bird corrects its aim. It points its beak where it knows the fish will be, not in the place it sees the fish.

Reflecting eyes

At night, when a car's headlights shine on the eyes of an animal, like a cat or a fox, that animal's eyes seem to glow. This is because the eyes of these animals have a membrane behind the retina that reflects light the way a mirror does. When rays of light reach the animal's retina, they stimulate its sensitive cells and are reflected back to the front of the eye to stimulate those cells again. Animals with this kind of eye can see well for night hunting.

Below: **The eyes of spotted hyenas appear here as dots of light. Hyena eyes reflect the smallest amount of light.**

SEEING COLORS

On the retina, cells called rods can see only shades of gray, which gives us black and white vision. Cone cells see colors; each cone sees a different one.

Some people can't tell the difference between particular colors (often green and red) because they don't have the cones that can see those colors.

Below: **Prisms break up sunlight into colors, but humans can see only some of them.**

These people are said to be "colorblind."

Birds and monkeys usually are able to see the differences between colors. Because they do not have cones in their retinas, however, many mammals can see only black and white.

Some animal species see in colored spots. The hedgehog can see yellow.

Invisible colors

Just as some animals can hear sounds that humans cannot hear, some animals are able to see colors that cannot be seen with the human eye.

A ray of sunlight seems colorless. But, if it is seen through a prism, such as the edge of a beveled mirror, the light breaks into bands of color — red, orange, yellow, green, blue, indigo, and violet — at least these are the colors the human eye can see.

Beyond violet are some ultraviolet rays that can dazzle us; for example, when the sun shines through clouds. These rays tan our skin and also can give us a sunburn.

Many insects do not see all the colors that humans see, but they can see ultraviolet rays. A bee can see blue and green, but not red. Bees see poppies only because they can see the ultraviolet rays these reflect. White flowers also reflect these rays.

Left: **The bee sees the ultraviolet rays this flower reflects, not its red color.**

Below: **If your eyes saw only polarized light, you wouldn't see the mountain reflected in the lake. Instead, you might see fish swimming.**

Straight rays

At the water's edge, indirect light from the sky makes reflections that can keep us from seeing into the water. Windows or mirrors also can reflect indirect light.

Indirect, or polarized, light travels in straight rays. Direct light rays go in different angles. We cannot see the difference.

Some animals, especially insects, can distinguish polarized light. Because these rays are straight, they can use them to find their way, even when the sun is behind clouds.

SEEING WITH DIFFERENT EYES

Above: **Because of the position of its eyes, the rhinoceros can see to the sides, but not in front.**

This way of seeing is called binocular vision.

This kind of vision gives predators an advantage when hunting for food. These animals, such as carnivorous mammals and birds of prey, have their eyes at the front of their heads, which gives them excellent binocular vision and a visual field that is straightforward. They can focus well on a single object, such as their prey.

Binocular vision

Each of our two eyes sees an image at a slightly different angle. To check this, close one eye at a time and look at some nearby objects.

When the two images are combined in the brain, we can then see in three dimensions — which cannot be shown in a photograph — and we can judge distances.

Monocular vision

Prey need to see danger from all directions. A wide field of vision helps them do this.

Herbivorous mammals, most birds, and many fish that are the prey of many predators have an eye on each side of the head. Each eye sees a single, different image. This is monocular vision, which gives animals a very large visual field, sometimes all around the head, as the woodcock has. Grazing animals, such as antelope and zebras, can see on both sides for predators. Fish also watch for enemies this way.

Left: **The woodcock's large field of vision can see everything around it.**

Large eyes

A globe-shaped eye has a larger visual field than an eye set deep in the head. The frog's round eyes set atop its head can see everything around.

The chameleon can move each of its bulging eyes separately. When it is hunting and sights prey, it focuses both eyes on the prey to accurately judge the aim of its long, fast-moving tongue.

Different directions

Research with birds has shown that the birds can be frightened by the mere silhouette of a predator if it seems to be moving toward the bird.

However, the same silhouette does not frighten the bird if it seems to be moving in a direction away from the bird. The bird no longer views the silhouette as a threat.

Below: **The chameleon can move each eye separately when hunting prey.**

GLOSSARY

algae — water plants with no roots, stems, or leaves.

amplify — to expand; to make larger or louder.

anemones — animals without skeletons that live in the ocean, usually attached to rocks and shells.

antennae — thin, jointed feelers on the heads of insects and crustaceans.

anus — the body opening which expels waste.

artificial insemination — the placing of an animal's male reproductive cells in a female animal body, usually by a human.

auditory — related to the sense of hearing.

bivalves — animals that have a shell in two halves, such as clams.

communal — the state of living in a colony or group where the members work together, like ants and bees.

crustaceans — animals that have a hard, outer shell and live mostly in water.

decoy — an artificial bird or animal used to take the place of the real creature.

elytra (*sing.* **elytron**) — the hard, protective wing covers of beetles and crickets.

facet — a single unit of a compound eye with a lens and light-sensitive cells.

filament — a fine, threadlike piece of material.

frequency — the number of sound waves per second.

glands — organs in the body that make and release substances such as sweat, tears, saliva, and poison.

lateral line — sensory organs, in a line down a fish's sides, which detect vibrations.

mate (v) — to join together (animals) to produce young.

membrane — a thin, flexible tissue layer in a plant or animal that lines or protects a certain part of its body.

mollusks — animals that have a hard, outer shell and usually live in water, such as clams and snails.

ocellus (*pl.* **ocelli**) — the small, simple eye of an insect, spider, or crustacean.

organ — a plant or animal structure made up of cells and tissues which have a specific purpose, such as an ear.

oscilloscope — an instrument that shows vibrations, such as from sound or electricity, as a visible wave form on a screen.

polarized light — light vibrating in a definite pattern, such as some rays of indirect light.

predators — animals that kill and eat other animals.

prey — animals killed and eaten by other animals.

proboscis — the long feeding tube, or tongue, on or under the head of some insects.

pupil — the opening in the vertebrate eye through which light passes.

reproduce — to create, or produce, offspring.

secrete — to form and give off a substance of some kind, usually liquid.

silhouette — the outline of an object with no visible interior details.

species — animals or plants that are closely related, often similar in behavior and appearance, and able to breed together.

spherical — shaped like a ball, or sphere.

tentacles — narrow, flexible parts or limbs that certain animals use for moving around and catching prey.

tympanus (*pl.* **tympani**) — a stiff membrane that vibrates to produce or receive sound.

BOOKS TO READ

ABCs of Bugs & Beasts. O. M. Day
  (Klar-Iden Publishing)

Amazing World of Night Creatures.
  Janet Craig (Troll Communications)

Animal Communications. Jeremy Cherfas
  (Lerner Group)

Animal Navigators. Jeremy Cherfas
  (Lerner Group)

Animal Senses. Jim Flegg (Newington)

Animal Vision. Jill Bailey & Tony Seddon
  (Facts on File)

Creatures That Glow. Melvin Berger
  (Scholastic)

Discovering Oceans, Lakes, Ponds & Puddles.
  Jeron A. Frame (Lion USA)

Exploring Our Senses series. Henry Pluckrose
  (Gareth Stevens)

Fish. Donna Bailey (Raintree Steck-Vaughn)

Interesting Invertebrates. Elaine Landau
  (Franklin Watts)

Jungle Birds. Anita Ganeri
  (Raintree Steck-Vaughn)

Mind-blowing Mammals. Leslee Elliott
  (Sterling)

Secrets of the Animal World series.
  (Gareth Stevens)

World's Weirdest Reptiles. M. L. Roberts
  (Troll Communications)

VIDEOS

Animal Sounds. (Encyclopædia Britannica
  Educational Corporation)

Animals Hear in Many Ways.
  (Phoenix/BFA Films & Video)

*Fish Senses & the Art of Underwater
  Photography.* (Environmental Media Corp.)

How Animals See. (Wood Knapp Video)

How Animals Talk. (Wood Knapp Video)

WEB SITES

www.bev.net/education/SeaWorld/walrus/
  phycharwal.html

www.wolf.org/referenc/faqs.html

www.wh.whoi.edu/homepage/faq.html

www.cnd.org:8013/Contrib/pandas/

INDEX

antennae 16-17, 19, 24, 30, 32, 36, 37
auditory canal 28, 29, 32, 34
auricles 32, 34-35

barbels 24, 25
bats 32, 33, 34, 35
bees 19, 37, 42, 43
binocular vision 44

caterpillars 30, 36
cats 22, 25, 34, 38, 41
cells 36, 38, 39, 41, 42
chameleons 45
cicadas 32
clown fish 14
cobras 29
cockroaches 30
colorblindness 42
colors 6, 7, 8, 38, 42-43
compound eyes 37
cones 42
crabs 16, 37
crickets 30, 31, 32
crustaceans 14, 16, 24, 30, 37

dogs 20, 21, 34
dolphins 34
dragonflies 37

eardrums 32
ears 26, 27, 29, 30, 32-35
earthworms 10, 36
elephants 25, 34
elytra 32
eyes 19, 33, 36, 37, 38-39, 40, 41, 42, 43, 44-45

feathers 32, 33
filaments 31
foxes 34, 41
frequencies 9
frogs 32, 33, 40, 45

grasshoppers 17, 30, 32

hearing 4, 5, 9, 27, 28-29, 30-31, 32, 33, 34
hyenas 11, 41

invertebrates 30-31, 38
iris 38

jackals 11
Jacobsen's organ 18

kiwis 10

lens 38, 39, 40
lions 5, 7, 22, 25
lobsters 16, 37
locusts 30, 32

membranes 32, 33, 41
moles 36
monkeys 24, 42
monocular vision 44
mosquitoes 17, 30
mussels 14
muzzles 24

navigation 34
nearsightedness 40
night vision 40-41

ocelli 36, 37
octopuses 24, 38
organs 14, 18, 19, 24, 32, 36
oscilloscope 9

osprey 4
ostriches 39
owls 32, 33, 38
oysters 14

peccaries 21
pigs 22
pike 12
polarized light 43
porpoises 34
predators 4, 5, 8, 13, 15, 44, 45
prey 4, 5, 18, 19, 24, 27, 29, 30, 31, 32, 34, 40, 44, 45
prisms 42
proboscis 19
pupil 38
pythons 19

rats 9, 42
rattlesnakes 19
reflections 41, 43
relationships 7
reproduction 6, 22-23
reptiles 18-19, 29
retina 38, 39, 41, 42
rhinoceros 44
rods 42

salamanders 36
salmon 13
scallops 15, 36
scent glands 17, 19, 21, 22
scents 6, 7, 10-11, 12-13, 14, 17, 18, 19, 20-21, 22-23
sea anemones 14, 15
sensitive hairs 30, 31, 32
sharks 29, 38
shrimp 16, 36

sight 4, 5, 36-37, 38-39, 40-41, 42-43, 44-45
smell 4, 5, 10, 11, 12-13, 14-15, 16-17, 18-19, 20, 24-25
snails 15, 36
snakes 18, 19, 29, 38 39
sound waves 9
sounds 5, 7, 8, 9, 26-27, 28, 29, 30, 31, 32, 33, 34
sparrowhawks 39
spiders 30, 31, 36, 37
squid 24, 38
sturgeon 24, 25

taste 4, 10-11, 15, 19
tentacles 14-15, 24
tongue 10, 18, 45
touch 4, 14, 19, 24-25
tree frogs 33
trout 39
trunk 25
tympani 32
types of eyes 44-45

ultrasounds 32, 34, 35
ultraviolet rays 42, 43

vertebrates 38-39
vibrations 25, 26-27, 29, 30, 31, 32
vipers 18, 19, 39
vultures 10, 11

webs 30, 31
whiskers 25
woodcocks 45

zebras 5, 45